I Am Sick

Written by Patricia Jensen

Illustrated by Johanna Hantel

My First
READER

children's press®

A Division of Scholastic Inc.
New York Toronto London Auckland Sydney
Mexico City New Delhi Hong Kong
Danbury, Connecticut

Library of Congress Cataloging-in-Publication Data

Jensen, Patricia.
  I am sick / by Patricia Jensen ; illustrated by Johanna Hantel.
     p. cm. — (My first reader)
  Summary: A sick child is afraid of going to the doctor, but when her father takes her and she takes her medicine, she begins to feel better quickly.
    ISBN 0-516-24878-2 (lib. bdg.)   0-516-24970-3 (pbk.)
  [1. Sick—Fiction. 2. Fear—Fiction. 3. Physician and patient—Fiction. 4. Physicians—Fiction.] I. Hantel, Johanna, ill. II. Title. III. Series.
    PZ7.J438Iam 2005
    [E]—dc22
                            2005004024

1 2 3 4 5 6 7 8 9 10 R   14 13 12 11 10 09 08 07 06 05

Note to Parents and Teachers

Once a reader can recognize and identify the 46 words used to tell this story, he or she will be able to successfully read the entire book. These 46 words are repeated throughout the story, so that young readers will be able to recognize the words easily and understand their meaning.

The 46 words used in this book are:

a	doctor	in	scared	too
already	ears	kids	scary	took
am	feel	looks	she	was
are	fever	medicine	sick	what
at	go	my	sneeze	will
better	have	need	that	you
buys	head	not	the	
cough	here	other	there	
Dad	hurts	rest	throat	
do	I	says	to	

My head hurts!
My throat hurts, too!

I cough.

I sneeze.

"You have to go to
the doctor," says Dad.

I am scared.

There are other kids here.

"Are you sick, too?"

What will the doctor do?

17

"You have a fever,"
says the doctor.

She looks in my ears.

She looks at my throat.

"You need to rest," says the doctor.

Dad buys my medicine.

"That was not scary!"

I took my medicine.

I feel better already!

ABOUT THE AUTHOR

Patricia Jensen lives in New Jersey. She has five children, three dogs, and is a stay-at-home mom.

ABOUT THE ILLUSTRATOR

Johanna Hantel has always been interested in art. She started drawing when she was still a young girl. When she is not illustrating, Johanna likes to spend time with her cat, Franklin, and run in marathons. Johanna lives near Philadelphia, Pennsylvania.